MW00897728

The Osage

by Janet Riehecky

Consultant:
Kathryn RedCorn
Director
Osage Tribal Museum
Pawhuska, Oklahoma

Bridgestone Books

an imprint of Capstone Press
Mankato, Minnesota

Bridgestone Books are published by Capstone Press
151 Good Counsel Drive, P.O. Box 669, Mankato, Minnesota 56002
http://www.capstone-press.com

Library of Congress Cataloging-in-Publication Data
Riehecky, Janet, 1953–
    The Osage / by Janet Riehecky.
        p. cm.—(Native peoples)
    Summary: An overview of the past and present lives of the Osage Indians, including a
description of their family life, government, the I'n-Lon-Schka ceremonial dances, and the
impact of the discovery of oil on the Osage reservation.
    Includes bibliographical references and index.
    ISBN 0-7368-1367-5 (hardcover)
    1. Osage Indians—History—Juvenile literature. 2. Osage Indians—Social life and
customs—Juvenile literature. [1. Osage Indians. 2. Indians of North America.] I. Title.
II. Series.
E99.O8 R54 2003
978.004'9752—dc21   2002002652

Editorial Credits
Tom Adamson, editor; Karen Risch, product planning editor; Heidi Meyer, book designer
    and illustrator; Alta Schaffer, photo researcher

Photo Credits
Carol Diaz-Granados, cover, 12, 14, 16, 18
Geneva Horse Chief, 10 (both)
Hulton-Deutsch Collection/CORBIS, 6
Immaculate Conception Church, 20
Osage Tribal Museum, 8

**The author wishes to thank Kathryn RedCorn and her family for their warm generosity
and hospitality during her visit to Pawhuska.**

1 2 3 4 5 6 07 06 05 04 03 02

Table of Contents

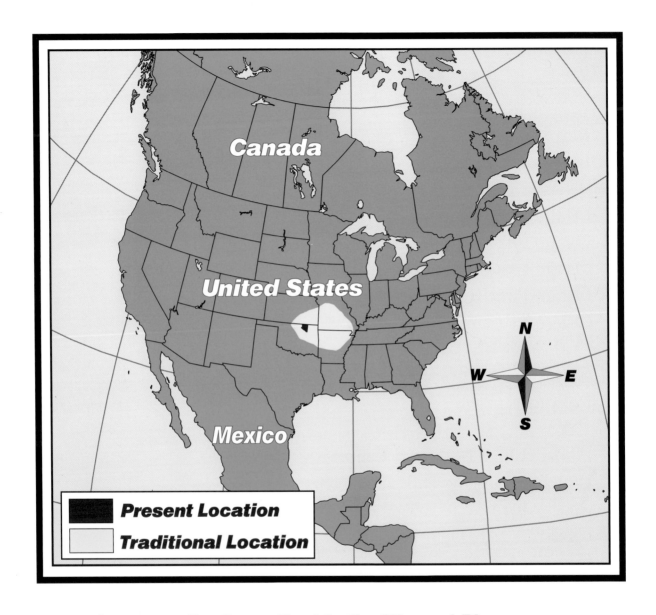

Long ago, the Osage lived in the Missouri River area.
They controlled much of present-day Missouri, Arkansas,
Kansas, and Oklahoma. Today, the Osage reservation is
in northeastern Oklahoma.

Fast Facts

Today, most Osage (OH-sayj) people live throughout the United States. Many Osage live on or near their reservation. Every June, hundreds of Osage return to the reservation for the ceremonial dances. The facts below tell about Osage history.

Homes: Traditional Osage homes are dome-shaped structures called wickiups (WIK-ee-ups). The Osage made a frame from willow or hickory saplings. They tied the saplings together with cloth strips. They then covered the frame with animal skins or canvas. Today, Osages live in modern houses.

Food: In the past, the Osage hunted buffalo, bear, and deer. They also grew corn, beans, squash, and pumpkins. Today, many Osages are ranchers or farmers. They also shop at modern grocery stores.

Clothing: Long ago, the Osage dressed in deerskin leather. Men wore leggings with a breechcloth. They added a leather shirt or robe in cold weather. Women wore wrap-around skirts with another leather cloth wrapped around the upper part of the body. Today, the Osage wear modern clothes, except for special ceremonies.

Language: The Osage language belongs to the Siouan language group. The Osage language is nearly extinct. Osage scholars are trying to bring back the language.

The Osage Name

The French traders who first met the Osage misunderstood their name. They thought the name for the People of the Water, Wazhazhe, referred to the whole nation. They wrote it in French as Ouazhigi or Ouasage (WAH-sah-gee). The British saw this word written on paper. They pronounced it OH-sayj. The name then became Osage.

6

Osage History

In the past, the two main groups of Osage were Sky People and Earth People. These groups were divided into smaller groups such as People of the Water and People of the Land.

The Osage lived in small villages throughout what is now the central United States. A wide dirt road ran east to west in each village. The Sky People lived north of the road. The Earth People's homes were to the south. Two chiefs ruled the village, one for war and one for peace.

In the 1670s, French traders visited the Osage. The Osage did not like the French at first. The French smelled bad and did not shave. But they eventually got along with the French.

For many years, the Osage kept their land and lifestyle. But in the 1880s, the U.S. government began forcing Indians on the east coast to move west. Many of them crowded onto Osage lands. Soon, white settlers moved west, seeking land for themselves.

This drawing shows what the Osage may have looked like in the 1800s.

Osage Oil

Beginning in 1808, the U.S. government persuaded the Osage to sign a series of treaties giving up their land. Eventually, they were forced onto a reservation in northeastern Oklahoma. They settled in the villages of Pawhuska, Gray Horse, and Hominy.

In 1894, oil was discovered on the Osage reservation. Osage leaders decided that the oil money would belong to the whole Osage nation. In 1907, they made an official list of 2,229 Osages. These people were called allottees. The allottees shared the money. The shares were called headrights.

Headrights could be split. If an allottee had four children, each child might inherit one-fourth of a share. A person could receive more than one share by inheriting from more than one allottee.

Many Osage were suddenly wealthy. But greedy people cheated them in business deals. Some men even married Osage women and killed them. They got away with the murder and the money.

The discovery of oil on the Osage reservation suddenly made the Osage wealthy.

The painting on the wall of the council meeting room is called a mural. This mural honors Osage culture.

Chief Charles Tillman Jr. stands next to the seal of the Osage nation. The pipe on the seal represents peace. The arrowhead stands for hunting and war. The gold color is for tribal prosperity.

Osage Government

Today, about 15,000 Osages live throughout the United States. About 2,000 live on or near the Oklahoma reservation. Two large groups live in California.

The Osage nation is governed by a principal chief, an assistant chief, and an eight-member council. They are elected to four-year terms by Osages over the age of 18. The chiefs and council members make decisions about Osage land and about the headright money.

Much of the oil is now gone. But descendants of the original allottees still receive money from their headright. The part of their headright decides how much money they receive. It also decides how much their vote is worth in an election. If a person has one-fourth of a share, that person has only one-fourth of a vote. If a person has three shares, that person has three votes.

Osage Family

The Osage feel that to be without a family is one of the worst things that could happen to a person. Osages care deeply about their immediate family. They also care deeply about all of their distant relatives.

The Osage language uses the same word for "mother" and for "aunt." In the past, an Osage woman treated her nieces and nephews like her own children. If something happened to their mother, she would raise them as her own. The Osage did not have a word for "cousins." They thought of cousins as brothers and sisters.

Most Osages try to stay close to all of their family members. They will stay in touch even if they move far away. Most Osages return to the reservation in June for a family reunion during the ceremonial dances.

Osage families try to have reunions during the ceremonial dances every June.

Osage Education

In the past, older members of the Osage nation taught children the traditions of their people. Boys were taught to be hunters and warriors. Girls were taught homemaking skills, including planting crops. The elders believed that a child learned best by watching others over a long period of time.

The U.S. government wanted the Osage to forget their traditions. They wanted the Osage to live the way white people did. In the 1880s, missionaries opened boarding schools. In 1884, the government passed a law stating that all Osage children between the ages of 7 and 14 had to attend these schools.

There were separate schools for boys and girls. Two of the schools were in Pawhuska, the capital of the Osage nation. Some of the children were sent to schools in other states. Osage parents did not like being separated from their children.

Older members of the Osage nation receive a great deal of respect. Young people seek out their wisdom and advice.

Sharing Traditions

In the mid-1880s, the Ponca and Kaw Indians brought their sacred ceremonial drum to the Osage nation. The Ponca and Kaw could not continue the drum's traditions. They taught their songs and dances to the Osage. The Osage considered this gift as both an honor and a responsibility. Both the drum and I'n-Lon-Schka dances are very sacred. People are not allowed to take pictures of them.

I'n-Lon-Schka

Every June since the mid-1880s, the Osage have held ceremonial dances centered around their sacred drum. The dances are called I'n-Lon-Schka (een-lown-ska). The name means "playground of the eldest son."

The dances are held over four days in the Arbor. This large building has a metal roof and is open on all four sides. Male drummers surround the drum in the center. Female singers sit in a circle around them. Male dancers sit on benches on all four sides of the dance floor. Female dancers and onlookers sit on bleachers around the outer edge.

Male dancers begin the dance. The men dance counterclockwise around the drum and the singers. They move their bodies and arms to suggest such things as a hunter or an eagle in flight.

Everyone stays in step to the beat of the drum. The women enter quietly after the men begin. They dance around the outer edge. As the Osage dance, they feel closer to each other and to God.

This Osage man is dressed for I'n-Lon-Schka. People are not allowed to take pictures of the dance.

Ceremonial Dress

To dance in I'n-Lon-Schka, a man must have traditional Osage dress. Men wear a breechcloth and leather or wool leggings tied to a decorated belt. They wear colorful silk shirts or vests. They fasten an otter pelt to the back collar, hanging it down straight. They also wear a scarf tied loosely around the neck. They attach bells below the knee. The outfit may be decorated with ribbons, silver medallions, and beads.

In the past, Osage men shaved much of their head, including their eyebrows. They left a strip of hair from the forehead to the back of the head. Today, the men wear a headpiece, called a roach, similar to the traditional hairstyle.

Women wear leggings of wool or leather and a skirt with a wide belt. They also wear a fringed blanket or shawl over a silk blouse. They decorate their clothes with ribbons, beads, and jewelry.

Osage men wear a roach made from deer tail hair. They make the hair stand straight up. They then attach an eagle feather to the top.

Religion

The Osage always have been religious. Their traditional stories tell of their worship of Wa-kon-ta, the Creator. They also asked for the blessing of Grandfather the Sun. They considered many animals to be sacred. The Osage prayed to borrow hunting or fighting skills from animals.

In the late 1800s, some Osage joined the Native American Church. This church combines Christianity with traditional beliefs. Christianity follows the teachings of Jesus Christ. Christian missionaries tried to convert the Osage. The missionaries often did not respect traditional Indian beliefs. But many Osage could identify with some Christian beliefs and chose to become Christians.

Today, most Osage belong to Christian churches. A beautiful Catholic church stands in Pawhuska. It is famous for its 22 stained glass windows. Pawhuska also has a Baptist church.

The Catholic church in Pawhuska, Oklahoma, is famous for its stained glass windows.

Hands On: The Hand Game

The Osage Hand Game is popular with Osage children and adults. It is a guessing game.

What You Need

10 sticks
4 buttons

What You Do

1. The game is played with two teams, the East side and the West side.
2. The object is to get all 10 sticks on your team's side.
3. Two people from the East side each hide a button in one of their hands.
4. A guesser from the West side tries to guess in which hand those players are hiding buttons. The guesser gets one guess for each button.
5. If the guesser is wrong with both guesses, the other team gets two sticks. If the guesser gets one right and one wrong, the guesser's team gets one stick. If the guesser gets both right, that team gets two sticks.
6. The teams take turns hiding buttons and guessing.
7. The game is over when all the sticks are on one side.

The Osage usually play five games. The team that wins the most games wins the match.

Words to Know

breechcloth (BREECH-kloth)—a piece of deerskin clothing that hangs from the waist

extinct (ek-STINGKT)—no longer living; an extinct language is one that is not used anymore.

inherit (in-HAIR-it)—to receive something from someone who has died

pelt (PELT)—an animal's skin with the hair or fur still on it

reservation (res-er-VAY-shun)—land owned and controlled by American Indians

sacred (SAY-krid)—having to do with religion

sapling (SAP-ling)—a young tree

tradition (truh-DISH-uhn)—a custom, idea, or belief that is passed on to younger people by older relatives or tribal members

wealthy (WEL-thee)—having a lot of money

Read More

Tallchief, Maria, and Rosemary Wells. *Tallchief: America's Prima Ballerina.* New York: Viking, 1999.

Wood-Trost, Lucille. *Native Americans of the Plains.* Indigenous Peoples of North America. San Diego: Lucent Books, 2000.

Useful Addresses

Osage National Council
P.O. Box 1449
Pawhuska, OK 74056

Osage Tribal Museum
819 Grandview
P.O. Box 779
Pawhuska, OK 74056

Internet Sites

The Osage Indians
http://www.uark.edu/depts/contact/osage.html
The Osage Tribe's Official Homepage
http://www.osagetribe.com

Index